One day closer to the harvest table!

Growing Your Own
Medical Cannabis in Soil

5

Core Concepts
of Cultivation Success
for the
Absolute Beginner

By **Sugary Tips & Friends**

Compiled and edited by **Michael Edward Browning**

Integral Education Press – Boulder, Colorado

i. e.
iNTEGRAL
eDUCATION
PRESS

Thank you for your purchase.

All proceeds from the sale of this title go to the ongoing expenses and efforts of Cinebis Film Institute. CFI is cinema committed to cannabis. Learn more about the role cannabis plays in our featured films and our global education mission at www.CinebisFilmFestival.com.

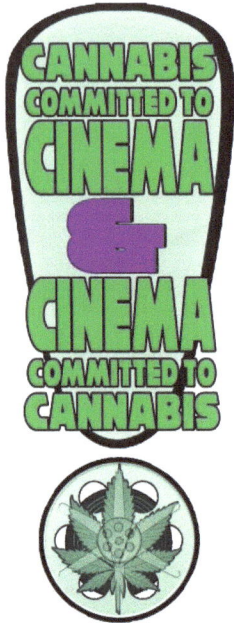

Integral Education Press
1750 – 30th Street, Boulder Colorado, U.S.A.

Book Design by Michael Edward Browning
http://michaeledwardbrowning.com

For information about exclusive discounts for classrooms, groups, or bulk purchasing options, please contact i.e. Press at (720) 772-9172.

Digitally manufactured in the United States of Cyberspace.

ISBN: 978-0-9758900-7-3

Library of Congress Cataloging-in-Publication Data

Tips, Sugary, et al., Browning, Michael Edward, Editor
Growing Your Own Medical Cannabis in Soil: 5 Core Concepts of Cultivation Success for the Absolute Beginner / Michael Edward Browning, Erik Burr, Hillary Carroll, Richard Maive, Daniel Phinney, Nikolaus Sanchez, Ian Stockdale, Sugary Tips

1. Gardening.
2. Cannabis.
3. Horticulture – How To.

For

all those

who are

embarking

on your

first season

of dancing

with this

beauty

Acknowledgements

With all his inborn eloquence, **Sugary Tips** came to me about a decade ago with a grand scheme of teaching thousands to grow medicine in their own spaces. He had grown his own, with the help of Cervantes' bible, for more than three decades already.

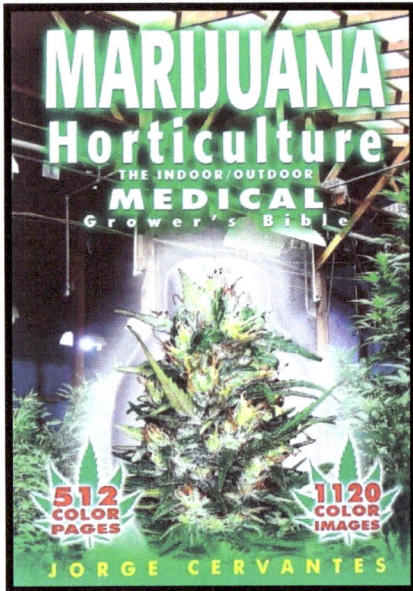

With many seasons comes considerable communication from *cannabis sativa*. In all his years as a carded patient caregiver in the backwoods of Oregon, one thing I can safely say about Sugary, he has learned to listen to his offspring.

If you only replicate one quality as a gardener, I would highly recommend working on your active listening skills. In communication with your plants, they will "tell" you what they need. It just takes time and experience to "hear" the indicators for what it is they specifically desire.

Albuquerque's **Anthony Ortiz** and his medical cannabis content team publish *Kurple Magazine*. The five core concepts presented here were culled from articles which originally appeared in Kurple while I was installed as editor/art director.

A tremendous advocate for Southwest medical cannabis patients, Ortiz has devoted his livelihood to sharing the goods in an educational way. Here, we'll continue that humane devotion. Thank you for publishing vital cannabinoid content, Kurple. You rock!

Each of the writers previously featured in Kurple is equally spot lit in this guide. Cumulatively, they have built a picture of what you absolutely need to know as a beginner.

1. **Daniel Phinney** gets us started with a simple, five-step game plan to foster your basic motivation.
2. **Rick Maive** sheds a little light on the lumen topic.
3. **Sugary Tips** floods readers with some vital H_2O "pHilosophy".
4. **Nikolaus Sanchez** moves us with his verbal ventilation on air flows.
5. **Hillary Carroll** and **Erik Burr** partner on how to partner with all the bugs and itty-bitties in your soil medium.

As a bonus, you'll also get **Ian Stockdale**'s inexpensive approach to your first hydroponic experiment.

Every grower has their favorite growing medium. Over time, you'll find one in particular, that grows on you. And *for* you.

Our biggest acknowledgement goes to the American (and Canadian) people who continue to lead the planet in pursuing the organic cannabis agenda for the benefit of all patients and peoples worldwide.

The fact that *every human and every mammal* have an endogenous Cannabinoid System means that *we all* have a stake in this conversation.

THANK YOU, for your purchase and for your participation in the process!

It's time for the talk.

And to get growing!

Michael Edward Browning
Summer 2018
Boulder County, Colorado

Every Human Has One

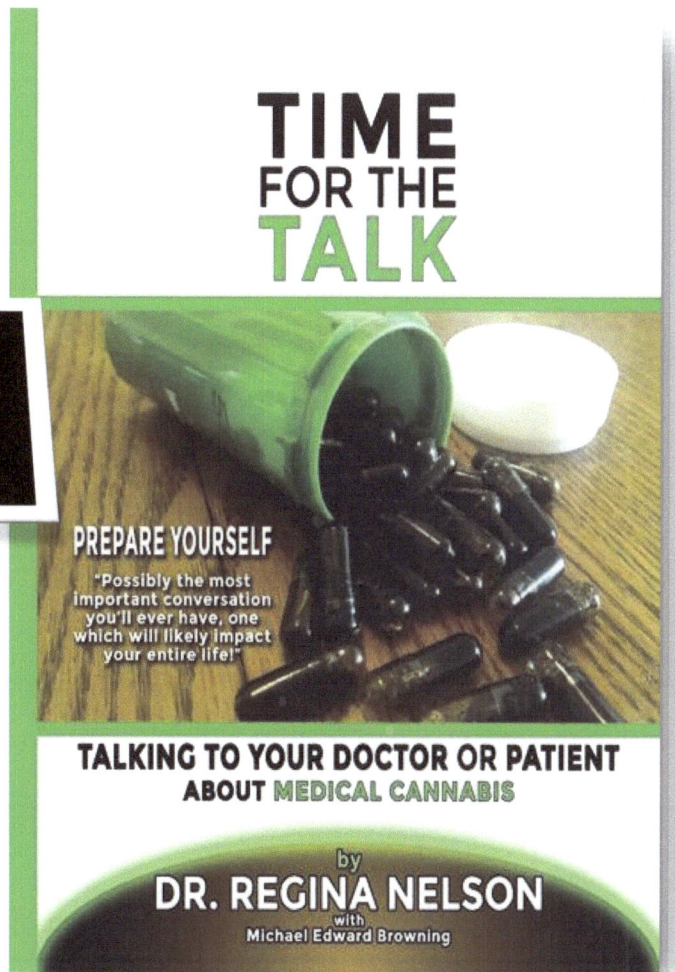

TIME FOR THE TALK

PREPARE YOURSELF

"Possibly the most important conversation you'll ever have, one which will likely impact your entire life!"

TALKING TO YOUR DOCTOR OR PATIENT
ABOUT MEDICAL CANNABIS

by
DR. REGINA NELSON
with
Michael Edward Browning

Introduction

This low-cost guide to growing medical grade *cannabis sativa* is prepared for the absolute beginner gardener. Here we share the very key core concepts of growing this herb that is already genetically driven to produce as many flowers as it can within the space of several weeks.

As you yourself grow on this journey of discovery, you will quickly outgrow the information presented here. However, as you develop your own knowledge base on each of these topics, you'll continue to refine your awareness of these five core concepts but never truly outgrow them - completely.

Action, light, water, air and soil health are the constituents that will yield your very own grown medicine in a short few months' time.

As your babies take root, I'd guess you'll notice a flowering in yourself as the weeks go by. For this is the other gift of gardening; mental, physical and emotional growth derived from your conscious action in support of an acknowledged life force.

Real time results are hard to ignore. It feels so good to watch a dear friend grow.

So (sew), get started!

Sugary Tips
Spring 2018
Oregon Highlands

Contents

You

The very most core of the five core concepts for the absolute beginner is to get the experiment underway, get your grow started!

Every season is a learning season for the home producer. Every day you spend around your plants is a day of increasing knowledge, increasing communication, increasing growth. Not just for the plant. It's kind of symbiotic.

As you know, it is called "weed" colloquially due to the humble fact that *cannabis sativa* simply wants to grow. As big as it can, as fast as it can. All we need do is *listen* to hear what kind of conditions will further that prime directive.

Any condition will produce results, it's when we understand how we can improve the conditions for our plants that we learn how to help them thrive. Effectively, we partner with them (and many more microbial associates) to create the optimal results from the (five) basic ingredients we are working with.

Besides these mentioned microbes, a subject which is infinitely complex, the basics are pretty basic: light, water and air (mostly moving it around). Put your seeds or starts into a moist medium with these three components and you're growing!

To get the absolute beginner started, we're going to assume that you have some genetic material (seeds or clones) and are ready to get growing today, now! For less than a hundred bucks, we'll get you in some good starting ground. For another hundred, we'll put a light on it – if you are growing indoors.

You can definitely spend piles of cash improving your grow, but you don't have to. Great results are possible with plants set directly into your yard and watered from your house hose.

There are thousands of things you can do to improve on that low-impact approach to cannabis husbandry, but it's not required.

A grow store owner from the Southwest shares an easy way to get things going. Five simple steps any patient can take to get started growing.

Shall we?

Learn more at Cannabinize.com

Motivation to Get Those Starts Or Seeds in Soil
By Daniel Phinney

The amount of gear needed to start your indoor or outdoor soil garden is simpler and cheaper than ever before these days. That alone should motivate you to get your hands dirty and get your own medicine growing!

With just these three basic products you'll be ready to produce good, usable medicine from each and every plant - with adequate time and lighting of course. More on that in the next chapter.

Get started today, nationwide, for less than $100 (in most cases). Here are the only five items you'll need to grow two plants to flower, besides your babies, of course!

- o 1 x Bag of Organic Garden Soil
- o 2 x 14-18" Black Plastic Saucers
- o 2 x 5 Gallon Fabric Pots [you can always trust the original Smart Pot™]

Keeping with a theme, there's only five steps to get your garden underway.

Simply...

1. Place one Fabric Pot on each of the Saucers
2. Fill each Pot with half the bag of Gardening Soil
3. Place your *clone* (a cutting off of another female cannabis plant) or *seed start* (baby cannabis plant) in the center of the Fabric Pot
4. Add water and light
5. Watch and listen to how they respond, then activate their environment

The most important aspect of growing your own medicine is to get started!

This easy, DIY approach helps even the helpless grow a green thumb! It's got a built-in backup plan so that if you do manage to off one of your upstarts, this setup is "made for two".

You can't grow wrong (in theory)!

Obviously, you can choose to add nutrients to your soil - usually by way of your watering solution. In this starter guide, we'll stay away from supplemental nutrient information. It's a very big and contested subject. We *will* talk acids and fungi.

After that, the plants will do what they do, which is grow. This chapter is about getting in the ground, digging in the dirt.

The first, most imperative measure you can take is to begin!

Hopefully you've started with a good quality potting soil. The extra aeration and root ball air pruning from the fabric pots combines with Humic Acid and plant protein hydroxylate in the soil to send your babies into their first frenzy of growth.

Cannabinize

Don't worry if those terms are not yet familiar to you. We'll cover much more on soil constituents in chapter five, but to keep things simple for the absolute beginner, just know that for the first few weeks *light and water* are the most important inputs.

They are still quite fragile at this stage and it's very easy to damage the little ones with "too much, too soon". A *nutrient burn* scenario is a real bummer to try and recover from early on.

Step gently into the realm of nutrients as you go thru your first season. It's a very easy place to misstep when you are just learning what your ladies require.

On the other side of your first adventure in gardening, you'll gain a wealth of knowledge, greater grower confidence and predictably, a few ounces of "happier" (with medicine you grew yourself). That first budding female will put the widest smile on your face as the fruits of your expended energy are reflected back at you.

With a little of that love, a little water and a little sun, this approach's sheer simplicity will have you producing like a master. Nice yields, potent plants and a fully natural, clean organic soil-grown, personally produced product await you.

One season's pre-packaged gardening experience for well under a hundred bucks.

Just add your clones or seed starts and get growing!

You can leave these on your patio or porch in full sun during the summer months and by fall you'll have a lovely bouquet of flowers.

Of course, the sun is the most sustainable source of illumination, but we'll also look at indoor lighting in chapter three.

Daniel Phinney *is one of the very knowledgeable owners of Hydro Lyfe, a cannabis farmer-friendly indoor growing supply store in Albuquerque.*

www.hydrolyfe.com

HYDRO LYFE grow shop.
albuquerque, NM

Light

No-Fuss Lighting Options for the Absolute Beginner
By Rick Maive

For first time growers, the choices available in lighting options can be daunting. Fluorescent, compact fluorescent, metal halide, sodium halide, high pressure sodium, induction, LED?

When setting out on your journey to choose the perfect light for your grow, you must take into consideration your space, ventilation and plant count.

If you plan to time your first garden experiment with the natural rhythms of the seasons, you can skip this chapter for now. The sun provides the most light power, the best light power and costs nothing. Utilize it if you can!

I prefer sun-grown medicine, but we all have personal parameters that will dictate the size, shape and location of our garden plots. Once you decide to grow indoors, you'll want a light source that suits your particular situation.

If you are first-time-ever growing with just a couple of clones, a simple T-5 Fluorescent array might be a great starter light for you (especially if your ventilation is limited).

This style is usually, truly plug and play, and should never get even remotely hot. However, you will never pull a pound of dry medicine from a plant under this light. While there's enough light to satisfy the full life cycle, there's just not enough of it to produce huge amounts of weight.

Once you are a bit more advanced, you might be ready to try your first ballast light and go for some serious medicine production. To get the best value, aim for a package of the three key components in a complete lighting system; ballast, bulb and reflector (also called a hood).

Be mindful of the effects created by entry level features like wing hoods (which can allow your room to heat up to undesired temperatures for your plants - if proper ventilation is not part of your environmental design). Some growers will intentionally use lights like this as a heat source for their grow rooms in the cold winter months.

The higher priced lighting systems include features that allow constant air flow throughout the interior of their closed hoods. This enables air to flow continuously around the bulb, keeping it cooler, in return allowing the grower greater ease in maintaining their grow room at a specific desired temperature.

A standard rule of thumb amongst indoor growers to keep in mind: when a grower maintains healthy plants, they can harvest an amount in grams similar or equal to the number of watts being used.

So, if you can afford it, you may want to purchase the amount of wattage output that you desire to harvest in grams of plant material at season's end.

1000 watts yields up to 1000 grams.

*This formula may not apply with lower wattage - but possibly greater resulting - LED options.

Entry level systems come as a base package featuring the ballast, reflector, and a 1000-watt bulb, but no ventilation is included in this setup.

That can become tricky, depending on your space. It is recommended that you speak to your local grow supply store for tips on constructing the proper ventilation system to go with your choice of lighting and space - in whatever climactic zone you reside.

You will find their localized guidance and advice invaluable to you on this journey of growth.

Additionally, the fourth chapter will serve as a spark to light your way when it comes to the "wind" in your garden.

Rick Maive has been loving the steady work in the cannabis garden for nearly forty years. He has successfully grown numerous signature strains to maturity in the various indoor-outdoor fluctuations of climate between OR, WA, CA, NV, NM, CO & OK.

Klaus James

Water

The ImpHortance of pH Levels to Cannabis Plants
By Sugary Tips

When considering environmental factors influencing the growth of plants, the pH of your water is one of the most important. Even (absolute) beginners can guess the environmental importance of light, temperature and moisture. But in order to rise to the higher levels of gardening accomplishment, one must consider the finer, more subtle influences: ones that our human senses cannot well discern.

Within any substance, pH is the measurement of acidity compared to alkalinity. This scale runs from the most acidic at zero and goes up to the most alkaline (or base) at 14. With cannabis, what you are looking for as ideal is about a 6.0 to 6.5 - right near the middle.

Neutral is considered to be 7.0. Therefore, ideal water for cannabis would be considered a slightly acid solution.

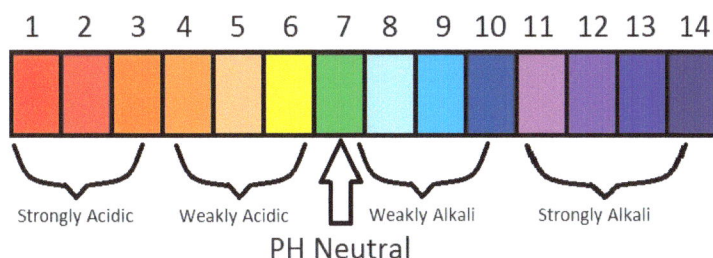

The pH scale is a logarithmic scale similar to the one used to measure earthquakes, called the Richter scale.

This means that the difference between 6.0 and 7.0 is actually ten times (x10).

| 1 | 2 | 3 | 4 | 5 | 6 | 7 | 8 | 9 | 10 | 11 | 12 | 13 | 14 |

Strongly Acidic   Weakly Acidic   Weakly Alkali   Strongly Alkali

PH Neutral

I was explaining this concept to a friend of mine the other day and he had one of those epiphany moments. He had been a pool maintenance guy and wondered why it was so easy to overshoot when you are adjusting the pH. Let's say you start out with really alkaline water, like I have, that clocks in around 7.8 to 8.4 (depending on how my well feels that day).

I give it a quarter cup of "pH down" adjusting solution and that might get me down into the low sevens. Then I add about half as much "pH down", and that gets me down to about 6.5.

So, to go from 6.0 to 6.1 is to double the alkalinity. From 6.0 to 6.2 is 3 times.

When your acceptable range is from 6.0 to 6.5, that is an enormous range, really, but occupies a relatively small niche in a very large spectrum.

Just a dribble at this point could push you down into the low sixes - where you want to be - but another drop or three and you're plummeting down into the low fives.

Why is this so impHortant?

A lot of plant metabolism has to do with the absorption of micro-nutrients which are dissolved in the soil or watering solution. The micro-nutrients cannot be dissolved and available to the plant if the pH is too far off their normal range.

This is very similar to how you see a drop-off in plant metabolism with the decrease or increase in temperature away from the optimal growing conditions range.

Just a 5° Fahrenheit shift in the temperature will cause a 20% decrease in metabolic rate. So, in my calculations, 10° equals 40% and 15° equals 60%. You can see how just small shifts in temperature, pH, moisture, etc. causes dramatic changes in the plant's ability to uptake nutrients.

After that lengthy lecture, the professor is getting around to telling you how to do it - and do it right.

First, I run my high iron and sulfur well water through a charcoal filter. Next, I add all the nutrients, supplements, stimulants, hormones and vitamins in my eight-part bloom formula. Interestingly, it is the addition of all these nutrients that bring the pH from that nigh onto eight range down into the high sixes.

One could correctly conclude that nutrients are relatively acidic.

pH Nutrient Availability

Earlier I mentioned that the optimal pH range for cannabis is 6.0 to 6.5. One experienced grower friend of mine insists on pH of 6.2 in his soil garden. I shoot for a 6.0 or even 5.9 because I know my solution is going to creep up in pH over the next few days. This has to do with the leaching of my soil-less hydroponics mixture, which is rich in coco fiber.

I irrigate twelve times a day with a slop hydroponics system that recovers all the water back into a large 36-gallon tank. It's a little like driving with bad alignment in a car where you always have to steer a little bit to the right.

Learn more at Cannabinize.com

The medium you employ has a greater effect on more than just how often you water and what types of pests you might find living in there. Over many years, I have developed a watering process and nutrient recipe that works for me in my desired medium.

It's best to start in soil and learn to communicate with your plants as a first step. As you develop your understanding of plant language, and your own level of activity in the garden, you will naturally customize your approach. It's understanding the concept of pH, acidity and alkalinity, that will help guide you in this process.

Sugary Tips is a West coast master grower from the hills of Oregon's Cascade Range, with more than a half century experience in cannabis cultivation. He spends most of his days of military retirement out in the Oregon sunshine (AKA rain) in communion with our favorite flora.

Learn more at Cannabinize.com

Air

Flow, Temperature and Atmospheric Humidity
By Nikolaus J. Sanchez

Maintaining your temperature and humidity is a very important factor when creating a total indoor environment. It will either positively or negatively affect your plants' growth by boosting or stunting their photosynthesis rate.

Even if it's your first time growing, it only takes a few simple steps to keep your gardens' air climate up to par.

Cannabis grows best with a consistent temperature range of 75-85 degrees Fahrenheit. This will encourage your plants to grow to their full potential with big sticky buds. Your girls will still grow in temperatures down in the 60's and up in the 90's, but those temperatures will most likely result in poor or moderate medicine.

The first step in maintaining air temperature in your home garden is to purchase a thermo-hygrometer. This device will not only read the temperature but also the humidity in your room.

Most thermo-hygrometers can be purchased for around $20. If you have a larger space, it is recommended that you purchase two or more.

If you are using low output lights, like a fluorescent T5 or an LED array, you should have no problem with them producing too much heat in your garden. However, if you are using a high intensity discharge (HID) light, additional steps will be required.

When setting the thermo-hygrometer up in your garden, be sure the probe is near the plants' canopy to give you an accurate reading of what the plants are feeling.

Air-cooled HID's will work best during the summer months. This will allow for the heat produced by the high intensity light to be pulled outside. If you are using an open hood HID, extra ventilation and air flow near the lights may be needed.

Also, some growers will run the "day cycle" during the night to help the temperatures stay a little lower when the lights are on; this is especially true with HIDs.

If you have tried ventilating your lights' heat and running them at night but your garden's temperature is still too high, you will want to purchase an air conditioning unit. These can be purchased for anywhere from $200-$700. Although it may seem a little pricy, you will see better results in production than when your room is too hot.

When purchasing an air conditioning unit, keep in mind that window mounted air conditioning is a thief's best friend, so a movable, portable air conditioning unit would be the best choice. Be aware that when bringing air conditioning into the garden it will raise the humidity level - so maintaining the humidity will be your next step.

With cannabis, the optimal humidity it desires changes throughout the plant's life.

During the vegetative or growth stage, optimal humidity levels are 40%-60%. When flowers start to produce or during the flowering stage, those humidity levels should drop to 30%-50%.

Letting humidity rise higher than 50% will increase the chance of fungus and mold while letting the humidity get too low in the room will slow down bud growth. However, for a beginner, keeping your humidity level between 30%-40% throughout the whole growth cycle will be acceptable.

In the desert Southwest, humidity levels are usually around 30%-50% depending on the time of day, which is perfect for cannabis growth. However, if you are using an air conditioning unit and/or it is monsoon season, humidity can easily jump higher than 50%. In order to lower the risk of mold and disease, a dehumidifier is imperative.

Dehumidifiers will filter the moisture from the air to help maintain optimal levels. When your plant's biosphere is in your own house, you must make the weather.

You can purchase a dehumidifier for approximately $200-$500. Again, this may seem a little pricy, but it will save your garden from nasty mold infections that could take out your whole crop overnight.

So inside, investment in the right equipment is imperative.

While this may seem like a simple factor of your total indoor environment, it's incredibly important to the success of your home harvest.

Nikolaus J. Sanchez is a photographer, gardener and all-around Renaissance man, living as an artist in New Mexico and traveling as a citizen of the world.

www.klausjames.com

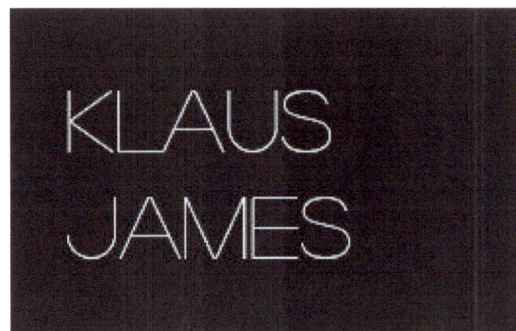

KLAUS
JAMES

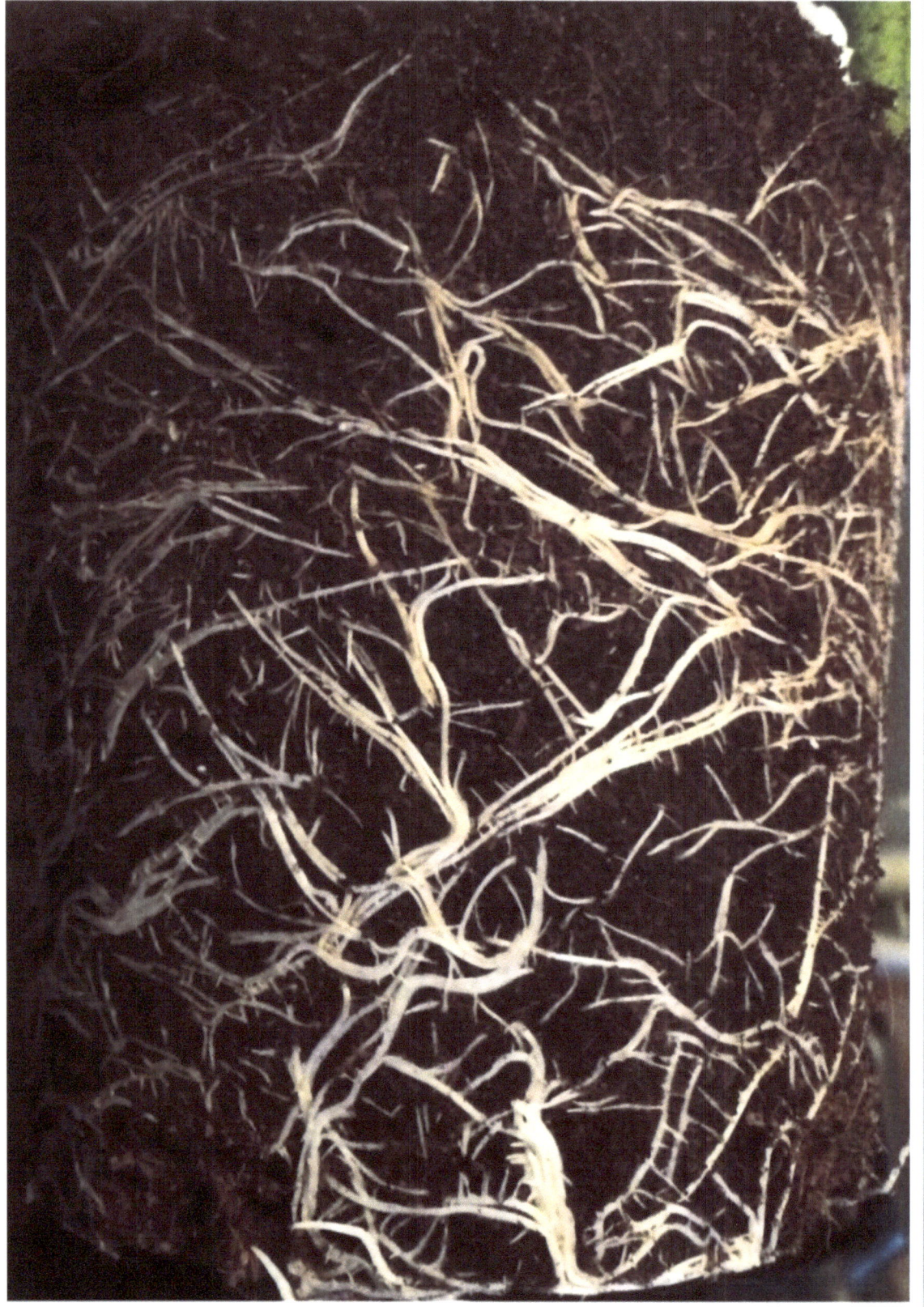

Learn more at Cannabinize.com

Soil

Inviting Friends to Help with Your Soil Food Web
By Hillary Carroll and Erik Burr

The soil provides the life force for any living plant; it is the stomach, heart, and brains of the plant. A nutrient depleted - or toxic - soil is going to create a sick and diseased plant. With plants, the first place to look for elements creating adverse conditions is at the soil level.

The roots of the plant communicate with the Soil Food Web by sending messages to special *fungi*, then down to *helper microbes* to provide the required nutrients and water.

Within a healthy soil, the messages are received by the helper microbes and the roots are provided with the substance that is in demand [*Editor's note: A function much like the two-way electro-chemical communication enabled by the Endocannabinoid System within our own human bodies.*].

These food and water packages are then sent up through the "veins and arteries" of the plant.

In an unhealthy - or nutrient depleted, possibly toxic – soil, the plant does not receive the needed "food" and water, thus progressing into a state of poor health, which can ultimately end with disease and death.

Here is the good news, a healthy soil can promote disease resistance, increase plant vitality, provide cost savings, and produce a better, more potent yield. Two important areas that are necessary for soil health are microbes / mycorrhizae and humic substances.

Microbes and Mycorrhizae

Most all plants form a symbiotic relationship with microbes in the soil, no different than the human stomach. Some have stronger relationships with bacteria, and others with fungi.

One of the most important of these fungi is *mycorrhizal fungi*, which requires the assistance of other beneficial bacteria and fungi within the Soil Food Web to achieve maximum benefits.

Remember that diseases of plants are actually the diseases of soil.

Much like trying to treat a human illness, the causative factor must be determined before a treatment can be prescribed.

The Soil Food Web is a community of organisms living all or part of their lives in the soil.

It is a complex living system and it interacts with the environment, plants, and animals.

There are two categories of mycorrhizae fungi; *endomycorrhizae* (endo=internal) and *ectomycorrhizae* (ecto=external).

About 90% of all the plants on earth have an association with these special fungi.

When a plant's roots have achieved high colonization of these fungi one sees improved nutrient and water uptake, disease resistance, drought resistance, improved soil structure, improved root health, increased root density, increased yields, and increased nutrient density of harvests.

These benefits can ease any grower's maintenance practices. Their abilities do not stop there! In the last two decades research has shown that mycorrhizae are responsible for building the precursor to soil fertility called humus.

Humic Substances

Humic substances are major components of humus, the end result of a biological and chemical process of decaying plant and animal matter. They are a collection of organic acids called *humic acids* and are made up of these main components: humin, *humic acid, fulvic acid,* and *ulmic acid.*

In this chapter we will focus on two of the components: humic and fulvic acid.

Humic acid is a principal component of humic substances. It is not a single acid; rather, it is a complex mixture of many different acids. Humic acid is known to influence the growth and proliferation of microbes but requires additional elements to achieve this microbial colonization.

It can help break up compacted soils allowing for enhanced water penetration and better root zone growth and development. It also adds essential organic material necessary for nutrient and water retention.

Plant growth is improved by the ability of the plant to gather and uptake more nutrients. Humic acid is especially beneficial in freeing up nutrients in the soil, making them available to the plant.

For instance, if an unusable aluminum molecule is bound with a needed phosphorus molecule, humic acid assists in detaching them and making the phosphorus available for the plant.

Humic acid acts as a nutrient, water, and oxygen "shuttle" assisting in the overall vitality of a plant's health.

Fulvic acid is a part of the humic acid molecule. It is an organic, naturally occurring electrolyte that can balance and energize cells.

Fulvic acid is active in dissolving minerals in a water-based solution. This is nature's way of *chelating* minerals - making them available for plant uptake. It also has the ability to change, alter, or combine with all other organic or inorganic matter.

Fulvic acid can often mobilize and transport many times its weight in dissolved mineral elements. It stimulates the metabolism of a plant to improve growth, reduce oxygen deficiency and enhance the immune system.

Fulvic acid stimulates and balances cells, increasing growth and replication conditions, which are vitally important to the health of the plant cells. Plants readily absorb high amounts of fulvic acid and maintain it in their cell and body structures.

As you see, there are many factors that contribute to soil health. The average person does not give much thought to what lives in soil and how it might affect the world around them.

If you are interested in growing plants whether for food, medicine, or decoration it is extremely important that soil health is your top priority. Without a healthy soil, a truly healthy plant cannot exist.

Like the living soil itself; we all need clean water, nutritious food, and the proper digestive bacteria and enzymes to be our healthiest selves.

Fulvic acid is also a natural free radical scavenger and natural antioxidant (plants, like humans, benefit from antioxidants!).

A free radical is a molecule that has extra electrons and becomes very reactive causing damage to surrounding molecules.

Fulvic acid can stabilize these free radicals.

Hillary Carroll and *Erik Burr* are the owners of *Nature's Force Organics*, an Albuquerque based manufacturer of organic, Non-GMO, and probiotic soil activation products for use in all cultivation industries.

www.naturesforceorganics.com

NATURE'S FORCE *organics*

Scientific Side Note

Cannabis Conversations Today April 27 2018 v1.1

During the 27th International Cannabis Research Symposium in Montreal I took a field trip to Ryerson University in Toronto to listen to Canadian scientist Steve Naraine on mammalian digestion-assisted seed dispersion.

Cool.

https://www.youtube.com/watch?v=Pa80_HxZfxk&t

A Wetter Appendix

My Minimalist Approach to Hydroponics
By Ian Stockdale

In the small-scale world of medicinal (and hobby) cultivation, it is the best time to be alive!

All of the resources to efficiently produce potent, clean, and tasty medicine are more than readily available. There are good grow stores all over the country, but with greatly varying prices and product lines it is hard to know the best route for beginners.

Being a minimalist, I stick to the bare bones basics to get from seed to finished product. I do it to save money, but I also do it because it's far more rewarding and fun to build your own system; to learn and understand hydroponics.

At the request of the editor I have put together an inexpensive, self-contained *Ebb & Flow* chamber, so you can understand hydroponics too.

Access to copious amounts of oxygen in the root zone makes plants healthy and explode with growth. Ebb & Flow has been around for a long time, because it's an effective, low maintenance way to grow, hydroponically. It is also very efficient, with a relatively small pump running at intervals, electricity usage is kept to a minimum.

The only real problem I have with Ebb & Flow systems is the cost of pre-assembled units. Even relatively small systems run upward of $250. I ran the numbers and, with $64 in my pocket, I began shopping for the perfect Ebb & Flow container.

The area I have is small, so the growing chamber itself has to be less than 26" long, about 18" wide, and cheap (less than $20). The container system would have two main plastic bins: one is deep, to perform the role of the reservoir; and one shallow, to act as the feeding tray (holding my precious starts).

The bins would have to nest tightly. The possibly perfect container: Modular Stackers from Sterlite. The containers' combined footprint, with width at about 16" and the length at around 25", is perfect.

I purchased the 19-gallon tub and the 10-gallon tub. They nest beautifully with enough room at the lip for the pump power cord to exit unobstructed from the reservoir. They were obviously made for this purpose!

All that was left was the pump and the plumbing fittings. The fountain pumps and 1/2" poly tube are available at any hardware store. I got a small, 48 gph (Gallons

Simply explained, an "Ebb & Flow" or "Flood & Drain" system uses a small pump to raise a nutrient solution from a reservoir into a tray for a set period of time (around 30 minutes) before draining back to the reservoir.

During the flood, stagnant air in the root zone is forced out of the growing medium.

During the drain, fresh air is pulled in around the roots.

Per Hour) submersible fountain pump for under $5 on sale and two feet of 1/2" clear poly tubing for about $2.

Luckily, pre-packaged "Ebb & Flow" fitting sets are at almost every grow store. So far, I had spent $18 on the tote bins and $21 on the plumbing fittings (Botanicare, Eco-Plus, etc.).

With a quick stop (at Hydro Lyfe) for expanded clay pellets, $17, and a dozen 5" square pots, I had $8 more poured into the project.

My $64 budget was broke, but I was stoked and ready for assembly!

DIY Ebb & Flow Hydroponics

Materials

   1- 19-gallon Modular Stacker (brown, never clear)

   1- 10-gallon Modular Stacker

   1- 48-92 gph submersible mini pump (*92 gph pumps must be turned down low)

   1- 24" section of 1/2" poly tube (clear plastic is preferred here, black is okay, but clear shows any clogs from roots)

   1- Ebb & Flow fitting set (recycled from swamp cooler drain parts, with some ingenuity)

   1- 10L-25L Bag of Expanded Clay Pellets, or grow stone, soaked and rinsed in 5.5 pH water

   2-12 square plastic pots (whatever suits your needs)

   8-10 gallons pH 5.5-6 water and complete, balanced hydroponic nutrients (General Hydroponics Flora series is a great starter)

   1- small light timer set to run for 30 minutes every 4-6 hours

Tools

   1- utility knife w/ fresh blade

   1- black marker

Assembly

A dozen 5" square pots fit perfectly in the shallow upper bin with just enough room for the standpipe and drain tube. Any size around pot that is 8" or shorter will work.

You can fit twelve little starts or as few as one or two bigger ones. Filling the bin directly with clay pellets or grow stone without the use of individual planting pots is effective as well, but it is harder to isolate plants. Once you have decided on your containers, place them in the shallow bin.

Based on the placement of your pots (and the pictures I provided to Cannabinize.com, surf there to see those shots and learn more) it will be obvious where to cut for your standpipe and drain.

To cut the holes for the standpipe and drain, use the threaded lock nut from the Ebb & Flow fittings as a template. Use the marker around the inside/outside of the lock nut. Taking care not to over-cut, use the utility blade to cut the holes to fit.

Place the fittings in the holes with the gasket on top. Tighten down the lock nuts. Attach one end of the poly hose to the drain/fill (not the taller standpipe) barb and the other end to the pump.

Place the pump and hose into the reservoir bin, keeping the cord out. Fill the reservoir bin with 8-10 gallons of prepared hydroponic water.

If mixing your watering solution up right in the bin, wait at least 30 minutes before running the pump for your dissolved solids and nutrients to mix thoroughly.

Transplant your plants carefully into the pots with the clay rocks and place them in the upper tray.

Set your timer, plug in the setup, and watch the magic happen.

If all this seems a bit too much for you to take on, I heartily encourage you to refer back to the first chapter on page 1.

There's something about soil when you're first getting started that's still satisfying many seasons later.

Now, get growing!

__Ian Stockdale__ is a professional hobbyist in the gardens of the god somewhere outside Santa Fe, NM. A cannabis environs experimenter from an early age, he has always maintained an organic ethic in his horticultural hijinx.

Encouragement

Well, now that you have a basic overview of cannabis cultivation, you can see how very simple (and very complex) it can be!

You really get to choose how much detail you wish to apply to your garden. Results, of course will vary, but you can almost rest *guaranteed* that you'll come out with something usable by harvest time.

Disasters do strike, but the plant itself wants to succeed.

It grows like a weed!

LEARN MORE

AND WATCH VIDEOS OF THESE

PLANTING PROCESSES AT

CANNABINIZE.COM

NOTES

www.ingramcontent.com/pod-product-compliance
Lightning Source LLC
Chambersburg PA
CBHW060834270326
41933CB00002B/81